A Dead Body in Taos

by David Farr

A Dead Body in Taos was first produced by Fuel and co-commissioned by
Fuel, Theatre Royal Plymouth and Warwick Arts Centre
with support from Bristol Old Vic.

The first performance took place at Bristol Old Vic on 30 September 2022 and
subsequently opened at Theatre Royal Plymouth on 18 October 2022,
Wilton's Music Hall on 26 October 2022 and Warwick Arts Centre on
15 November 2022, in a production supported by Arts Council England, the
Wellcome Trust, the Esmée Fairbairn Foundation and the Turing Institute.

A Dead Body in Taos

by David Farr

Cast

LEO   David Burnett
JACOB FELLOWS   Nathan Ives-Moiba
SAM   Gemma Lawrence
TRISTANA CORTEZ/AGNES MARTIN/KATH'S MUM   Clara Onyemere
KATH   Eve Ponsonby
CURTIS ADAMS/MICHAEL/DR FRITZ ERHARDT   Dominic Thorburn

All other parts played by members of the company

Creative Team

Director   Rachel Bagshaw
Designer   Ti Green
Lighting Design   Katy Morison
Composition and Sound Design   Ben and Max Ringham
Video Design   Sarah Readman
Movement Director   Ingrid Mackinnon
Accent Coach   Gurkiran Kaur
Costume Supervisor   Victoria Nissley
Assistant Directors   Tian Brown-Sampson, Oliwia Charmuszko-Carrigan
Associate Sound Designer   Ellie Isherwood
Assistant Costume Supervisor   Jo Lewis
Casting Director   Louis Hammond CDG
Production Manager   Helen Mugridge
Company Stage Manager   Roisin Symes

Thanks

Nick at Centreline Fabrications, Nick and Nick at London Theatre Company, Tom Morris, Dr Magda Osman, Adam Curtis, and the Arcola Theatre.

David Burnett | Leo

Theatre includes: *Macbeth* (Chichester Festival Theatre); *The Point of It* (RADA Festival); *Antony and Cleopatra* (RSC); *Titus Andronicus, Julius Caesar* (RSC); *Britten in Brooklyn* (Wilton's Music Hall); *Brave New World* (Royal and Derngate); *Faust* (UK tour); *Gate 35* (Gate Theatre); *Family Tree* (Theatre503); *Pioneer* (Norwich Playhouse); *The Best Years of Your Life* and *Jefferson's Garden* (Watford Palace Theatre).

TV includes: *The Baby* (Sky/HBO); *Call the Midwife* (BBC); *Victoria, Manhunt* and *Endeavour* (ITV).

Film includes: *The Mummy* (Universal Pictures).

Nathan Ives-Moiba | Jacob Fellows

Nathan trained at LAMDA.

Theatre includes: *Dictating To The Estate* (Special Measures); *All My Sons* (Queen's Theatre); *Who Killed Alfred Oliver?, The Last Abbot of Reading* (Rabble Theatre); *A Midsummer Night's Dream, And Did Those Feet, Tull* (Octagon Theatre); *Macbeth* (GSC); *Hay Fever* (Citizens Theatre/Royal Lyceum Theatre); *Archipelago* (Lighthouse Theatre); *Soul* (Hackney Empire/Royal & Derngate); *As You Like It* (National Theatre); *My Children My Africa* (Trafalgar Studios); *Jekyll & Hyde* (Selladoor); and *Our Country's Good* (Out of Joint).

TV includes: *Roadkill, Doctors* (BBC); *The Awoken* (Sky Vision); *Salting the Battlefield* (Carnival Films/BBC); and *Coronation Street* (Granada Television).

Film includes: *Outdoors* (Grey Moth); *Tuesday* (A24/BBC Film); *Edward II* (Relative Motion); *The Flood* (Megatopia Films); *Growing Pains* (FIKSA); *Luise Rainer, I Can See Into Next Door's Garden* (Leering Falcon); and *Young Radicals* (LAMDA).

Radio includes: *The Minister of Chance* (Radio Static).

Nominated Best IDEA Production OffWestEnd Awards (*Dictating To The Estate*); nominated Best Newcomer Manchester Theatre Awards 2014 (*Tull*); nominated Best Supporting Male OffWestEnd Awards 2016 (*My Children My Africa*).

Gemma Lawrence | Sam

Credits as a writer and actor include her OFFIE-nominated debut play *Sunnymead Court* (Arcola Theatre/Actor's Centre/UK tour). Other theatre includes: *Anything is Possible if You Think About It Hard Enough* (Southwark Playhouse); *Not Talking* (Arcola Theatre); *Five Plays: Nuclear* (Young Vic); *Wasted* (Orange Tree Theatre); *All My Sons* (Hong Kong Arts Festival); *The Tempest* (Southwark Playhouse); *As You Like It, Children of the Sun* (National Theatre); *Much Ado About Nothing* (Shakespeare's Globe); *Gaslight* (Salisbury Playhouse); *Lee Harvey Oswald* (Finborough Theatre); *The Cherry Orchard* (Bristol Tobacco Factory, Rose Theatre); and *Rough Cuts: The Lion's Mouth* (Royal Court Theatre).

TV includes: *Silent Witness, Shakespeare and Hathaway, 18 – Clash of Futures, Luther, Misfits, 1066, Waking the Dead, Time of Your Life, Stir it Up, All About George* and *Ahead of the Class.*

Film includes: *Frail, A Bunch of Amateurs* and *Enlightenment.*

Clare Onyemere | Tristana Cortez / Agnes Martin / Kath's Mum

Clara is a co-founder of Immediate Theatre.

Theatre includes: *Youth Without God* (Coronet Theatre); *Risk Assessment* (RADA Festival); *Mary Wollstonecraft* (Unitarian Church); *Pandora's Box, Masks* (Ovalhouse Theatre); *Private Thoughts* (Theatre Ortas); *Chicken* (Hackney Empire); *Unstated* (Red Room); *Richard III* (Southwark Playhouse); *Orestes* (Shared Experience); *Six Acts of Love* (Tron Theatre); *Yerma* (Collective Artistes); *Uncle Vanya* (Babel Theatre); *King, Witch* (Watermill Theatre); *Duet for One* (Bury St Edmunds Theatre Royal); *All's Well*

That Ends Well (Oxford Stage Company); *Snow Queen* (Manchester Library); *Macbeth* (New York Theatre Festival); *Blood Wedding* and *Fuente Ovejuna* (National Theatre).

TV and film includes: *Casualty*, *Sitting in Limbo*, *Liar*, *Breeders*, *MotherFatherSon*, *Our Girl*, *Wolfblood*, *Come Home*, *Motherland*, *Lucky Man*, *Cuffs*, *The Five*, *iboy*, *Molly*, *Holby City*, *Law and Order*, *Criminal Justice*, *The Bill*, *Doctors*, *Eastenders*, *Out of the Blue* and *The Tomorrow People*.

Eve Ponsonby | Kath

Theatre includes: *Little Scratch* (Hampstead Theatre); *Sadness and Joy in the Life of Giraffes* (Orange Tree Theatre); *Harry Potter and the Cursed Child*, *Shakespeare in Love*, *The Children's Hour* (West End); *Al Love You* (VAULT Festival); *A Midsummer Night's Dream* (Theatre Royal Bath); *Little Eyolf* (Almeida); *'Tis Pity She's a Whore* (Cheek by Jowl); *If Only* (Chichester Festival Theatre); *Longing* (Hampstead Theatre); *Boys* (Headlong); *Hamlet* (Shakespeare's Globe); and *Prince of Denmark* (National Theatre/NYT).

TV includes: *Sliced* (Dave); *Carnival Row* (Amazon); *Grantchester* (Lovely Day/ITV); *Lady Chatterley's Lover*, *The White Queen* (BBC); *Misfits* (Clerkenwell Films); *Above Suspicion* and *Silent Scream* (ITV).

Film includes: *Frankenstein* (20th Century Fox); and *The Unbeatables* (369 Productions).

David Thorburn | Curtis Adams / Michael / Dr Fritz Erhardt

Dominic Thorburn trained at Drama Centre London.

Theatre includes: Kenneth Branagh's *Macbeth* (UK and New York); *One Man, Two Guvnors* (National Theatre in the West End); *Our Country's Good* (Out Of Joint); Sir Peter Hall's *Henry IV I & II* (Theatre Royal Bath); *A Month in the*

Country (Gate Theatre, Dublin); *Henry V*, *The Winter's Tale* (Propeller). Most recently Dominic appeared in *Tom, Dick & Harry* (New Vic Theatre and Alexandra Place).

TV and film includes: *A Dangerous Fortune*, *Our World War*, *Endeavour*, *EastEnders* and *Rebellion*.

Dominic also regularly voices commercial campaigns for global brands and numerous high profile video games, TV shows and audiobooks.

David Farr | Playwright

David Farr is a playwright, screenwriter, stage director, novelist and film/TV director whose plays have been performed all over the world. He has increasingly moved into film and television, working on the long-running BBC show *Spooks* and completing his first feature film, *Hanna*, for Focus Features in 2009. His directorial debut, *The Ones Below*, with Cuba Pictures, premiered at Toronto International Film Festival in 2015 and was released in UK cinemas in March 2016.

David's adaptation of John le Carré's novel *The Night Manager*, produced by The Ink Factory, starring Hugh Laurie and Tom Hiddleston and directed by Susanne Bier, aired on BBC1 in 2016. A total of 9.9 million people tuned in to watch the series finale and the show earned multiple awards and nominations.

David's episode of the Philip K. Dick series *Electric Dreams*, entitled *Impossible Planet*, aired on Channel 4 in 2017 and his BBC1 and Netflix epic miniseries *Troy: Fall of a City* aired in February 2018. David adapted his feature film *Hanna* into a television series for Amazon Prime. Series 2 of *Hanna* was released to great praise in 2020, with David writing and directing. Series 3, the final series of *Hanna*, was released in 2021. Most recently David's adaptation of *The Midwich Cuckoos* produced by Route 24 was released on Sky.

David's theatre career began when he became Artistic Director of the Gate Theatre, London, in 1995. His work at the Gate earned him a reputation as one of the most exciting new talents in British theatre, a reputation that he built on when he left the Gate to become Artistic Director of Bristol Old Vic in 2002, and London's Lyric Theatre, Hammersmith, in 2005.

In 2009, David left the Lyric to become Associate Director of the Royal Shakespeare Company. His productions, *The Winter's Tale*, *King Lear* and *The Homecoming* all opened to critical acclaim.

David's first book for children, *The Book of Stolen Dreams*, was published in hardback in 2021 and in paperback in September 2022.

Rachel Bagshaw | Director

Rachel is an award-winning stage director and is Associate Director at the Unicorn Theatre.

Recent productions include: *Augmented* by Sophie Woolley (Royal Exchange/Told by an Idiot) and *Philip Pullman's Grimm Tales* (Unicorn Theatre Online).

Other work includes: *The Bee in Me* and *Aesop's Fables* (Unicorn Theatre); *Midnight Movie* (Royal Court Theatre). Her critically acclaimed work *The Shape of Pain* won a Fringe First at Edinburgh, was revived at Battersea Arts Centre in 2018. Other productions include: *Resonance at the Still Point of Change* (Unlimited Festival, South Bank Centre); *The Rhinestone Rollers* and *Just Me, Bell* (Graeae).

Film includes: *Let Loose* (Unicorn Theatre Online/ENB) and *Where I Go* (*When I Can't be Where I Am* (BBC/China Plate). She is an Associate Artist at Wilton's and works extensively in engagement and young people's work.

Ti Green | Designer

Recent work includes: *Touching the Void* (Duke of York's, Bristol Old Vic); *Cyrano*

de Bergerac (Bristol Old Vic); *Bartholomew Fair* (The Globe); Rogers and Hammerstein's *Cinderella* (Sevenages, Shanghai Culture Square and tour of China); *What Shadows* (Birmingham Rep/Edinburgh Lyceum/Park Theatre, London); *The Emperor* (Young Vic/HOME/TFANA New York); *The Government Inspector* (Birmingham Rep and national tour); *The Funfair* and *Romeo and Juliet* (HOME, MTA winner for Best Design); *Playing for Time* (Sheffield Crucible); *Bright Phoenix* (Liverpool Everyman); *A Christmas Carol* (Birmingham Rep); *Orlando* (Manchester Royal Exchange); *Henry VI, Parts I, II & III* (Shakespeare's Globe); *Time and the Conways* (Royal Lyceum Theatre Edinburgh/ Dundee Rep, CATS nomination for Best Design); *Unleashed* (Barbican) and *The Resistible Rise of Arturo Ui* (Liverpool Playhouse).

Designs for the National Theatre: *Revenger's Tragedy*, *The Five Wives of Maurice Pinder*, *The UN Inspector*, *Coram Boy* (National Theatre/Imperial Theatre New York, Tony nominations for Best Costume and Set Design). For the RSC: *Richard III*, *Little Eagles*, *Coriolanus*, *Dido Queen of Carthage and Julius Caesar*.

Katy Morison | Lighting Designer

Katy is an experienced Lighting Designer working throughout the UK, across a variety of productions.

Recent productions include: *Hero of the People, The Snow Queen, Alice in Wonderland* (Sherman Theatre); *Possible* (National Theatre Wales); *A Tale of Two Cities* (Lost Dog); *The In Between* (Theatre Clwyd/National Youth Arts Wales); *ANTHEM* (Wales Millennium Centre); *The Glee Club* (Kate Wasserberg/Out of Joint UK tour); and *The Violence Series* (The Other Room).

She is a lecturer and supervisor at the Royal Welsh College of Music and Drama and was part of lighting team at Sherman Theatre for many years. Katy has worked as an Associate Designer and re-lighter for major productions and renowned lighting designers.

Ben and Max Ringham | Composition and Sound Design

As writers: *Exemplar* (BBC Radio 4 Series); *Looking for Nigel* (BBC R and D); *Many Ghosts* (2 Temple Place, as co-creators); *Anna* (National Theatre); *The Crackles* (Shoreditch Town Hall); *Monument* and *Discount Disco* (Wiretapper London).

As composers/sound designers: *Blindness, Belleville, Teenage Dick, Piaf, Berberian Sound Studio* (Donmar Warehouse); *Cyrano de Bergerac* (Drama Desk Awards Best Sound Designer Winner); *Betrayal* (Pinter at the Pinter with the Jamie Lloyd Company); *Tartuffe, Ugly Lies the Bone, We Want You to Watch, Scenes from an Execution, Henry IV, Parts I & II, She Stoops to Conquer, The World of Extreme Happiness* (National Theatre); *A Mad World My Masters, Queen Anne, Little Eagles* (RSC); *Machinal* (Almeida); *The Mighty Walzer, Parliament Square, Our Town* (Royal Exchange); *Gloria, The Haystack* (Hampstead); *Pygmalion* (Headlong); *Killer* (Off-Westend Awards Best Sound Designer Winner); and *The Pitchfork Disney* (Shoreditch Town Hall).

Sarah Readman | Video Designer

As lighting and video designer, previous work includes: *Endurance* (Jenny Jackson); *Everyman* (Miracle Theatre); *Antigone* (LAMDA); *Midnight Movie* (Royal Court, with Joshua Pharo); *How to Save the Planet* (Unlimited Theatre); *Bystanders* (Cardboard Citizens); *Future Bodies* (RashDash, with Joshua Pharo).

As video designer: *The Crucible, This Beautiful Future* (Yard Theatre).

As lighting designer: *Let Loose* (Unicorn Theatre); *Dirt, WOW EVERYTHING IS AMAZING, Fire in the Machine, Phenomena: A Beginner's Guide to Love and Physics* (Sounds Like Chaos); *Voodoo*

(Project O); *Dark Earth* (Wiretapper); *Kabeiroi* (Punchdrunk); *punkplay* (Southwark *Playhouse); The Owls Are Not What They Seem* (Lemonade and Laughing Gas); and *Shelter Me* (Circumference).

Ingrid Mackinnon | Movement Director

Ingrid Mackinnon is a London based movement director and choreographer.

Movement direction includes: *The Darkest Part of the Night, Girl on an Altar* (Kiln Theatre); *Playboy of the West Indies* (Birmingham Rep); *The Meaning of Zong* (Bristol Old Vic/UK tour); *Moreno* (Theatre503); *Red Riding Hood* (Theatre Royal Stratford East); *Antigone* (Mercury Theatre); *Romeo and Juliet* (Regent's Park Open Air Theatre, Winner Black British Theatre Awards 2021 Best Choreography); *Liminal – Le Gateau Chocolat* (King's Head Theatre); *Liar Heretic Thief* (Lyric Hammersmith); *Reimagining Cacophony* (Almeida Theatre); *First Encounters: The Merchant Of Venice, Kingdom Come* (RSC); *Josephine* (Theatre Royal Bath); *Typical* (Soho Theatre); *#WeAreArrested* (Arcola Theatre and RSC); *The Border* (Theatre Centre); *Fantastic Mr. Fox* (as Associate Movement Director, Nuffield Southampton and National/International tour); *Hamlet, #DR@CULA!* (Royal Central School of Speech and Drama); and *Bonnie & Clyde* (UWL: London College of Music).

Other credits include: intimacy support for *Antigone, 101 Dalmatians, Legally Blonde, Carousel* (Regent's Park Open Air Theatre), and intimacy director for *Girl on an Altar* (Kiln Theatre).

Louis Hammond CDG | Casting Director

Theatre includes: *The Strange Undoing of Prudencia Hart* (Royal Exchange, Manchester); *Barber Shop Chronicles* (Fuel/Roundhouse/UK tour/BAM New York); *The 5 Plays Projects* (Young Vic); *Beautiful Thing, Macbeth* (Tobacco Factory, Bristol); *Heroine, Kanye the First*

(HighTide Festival); *The Sugar-Coated Bullets of the Bourgeoisie* (Arcola/HighTide Festival); *Inkheart* (HOME Manchester); *The Distance* (Sheffield Crucible/Orange Tree Richmond); *Romeo and Juliet* (Sheffield Crucible); *Harrogate* (HighTide Festival/Royal Court); *Creditors* (Young Vic); *The Funfair* (HOME Manchester); *Primetime, Violence and Son, Who Cares, Fireworks* (all as Casting Associate at the Royal Court); *Romeo and Juliet* (HOME Manchester); *Amadeus* (Chichester Festival Theatre); *The Winter's Tale* (Regent's Park Open Air Theatre); *The History Boys* (Sheffield Crucible); *Driving Miss Daisy (UK tour); Batman Live* (world arena tour), *The Trial of Dennis the Menace* (Southbank Centre); *The Resistible Rise of Arturo Ui* (Liverpool Playhouse/Nottingham Playhouse); *Blue/Orange* (Arcola); *Von Ribbentrop's Watch* (UK tour); *Mrs Reynolds and The Ruffian, Brighton Beach Memoirs, Absent Friends* (all Watford Palace); *All My Sons* (Curve, Leicester); 50th Anniversary Season of 50 Rehearsed Readings, Caryl Churchill Season, International Residencies and new writers' Rough Cuts presentations (all Royal Court); *The Member of the Wedding, Dirty Butterfly, The Indian Wants the Bronx* (all Young Vic); *Loot* (Tricycle Theatre); *Blowing Whistles* (Leicester Square Theatre); *Testing the Echo* (Tricycle Theatre/Out of Joint tour); *The Importance of Being Earnest* (UK tour/Vaudeville); *Donkeys' Years* (UK tour); *Rock'n'Roll* (Royal Court/Duke of York's); and *Jus' Like That* (Garrick).

TV includes: Head of Casting at *The Bill* (Thames TV).

Film includes: *Arsene Lupin, Ne Quittez Pas, Beyond Re-Animator, Mirrormask, Olve.*

Louis Hammond is a member of the Casting Directors' Guild of Great Britain and Ireland.

About Fuel

Fuel leads the field in independent producing in the UK's live performance sector, working with brilliant artists to explore urgent questions, to shine light on how we relate to each other and the world around us, and to tell untold stories by under-represented voices. Fuel produces high-quality new theatre that reaches diverse audiences through tours to venues in the UK and internationally, collaborating with outstanding theatre-makers with fresh perspectives and approaches who produce shows, performances or experiences which have direct and playful relationships with their audiences.

Fuel is celebrated for its pioneering producing model that develops innovative ideas through attentive collaboration, a spirit of curiosity, and an emphasis on trust, and has developed a reputation for spirited and surprising new theatre, deep relationships with a wide range of artists, and passionate commitment to inclusion and care for young and diverse audiences.

Fuel was founded in 2004 and is led by Kate McGrath. Since its story began, Fuel has produced shows, festivals, films, installations, podcasts, apps and books. In doing so, Fuel has supported the artistic development of over 120 lead artists or companies and reached more than a 1.5 million people, live and digitally, hosted over a hundred internships and been recognised with awards for its work. Fuel is currently working with artists and companies including Will Adamsdale, Travis Alabanza, Common Wealth, Inua Ellams, ESKA, Lewis Gibson, Alan Lane, Hannah Lavery, Pauline Mayers, Racheal Ofori, Toby Olié, Hema Palani, Jenny Sealey, Melly Still, Keisha Thompson, Uninvited Guests and Melanie Wilson.

Fuel is supported by Arts Council England as a National Portfolio Organisation, Fenton Arts Trust, the Garrick Trust, the Backstage Trust, the Esmée Fairbairn Foundation, the Paul Hamlyn Foundation, and the Garfield Weston Foundation.

About Theatre Royal Plymouth

Theatre Royal Plymouth (TRP) is a registered charity providing art, education and community engagement in Plymouth and across the region. It engages and inspires with the aim of touching lives. Theatre Royal Plymouth presents a year-round programme of world class productions on all scales as the South West's principal centre for performing arts.

Theatre Royal Plymouth works with partners to understand the challenges people face accessing the arts, especially vulnerable and disadvantaged people. It creates pathways that are genuinely accessible to those who might otherwise never get to engage with the arts. They collaborate to co-create and co-author work that represents the community, creating the space needed for people to tell their story in their own way.

Theatre Royal Plymouth is the UK's largest regional producing theatre. With a focus on embracing the vitality of new talent and supporting emerging and established artists. It collaborates with a range of partners to provide dynamic cultural leadership for the city of Plymouth.

About Warwick Arts Centre

One of the largest multi-artform venues in the UK, Warwick Arts Centre delivers a high quality, engaging, and diverse programme of performing and visual arts, concerts, films, festivals, education and learning activities, and special events – all presented in world-class venues and spaces.

Since opening in 1974, the venue – at the heart of Coventry's University of Warwick campus – has been a distinctive and special place, an important resource for both the arts and audiences in the region, as well as a significant force in national and international arts networks.

About Wilton's Music Hall

Wilton's is a Grade II* building of international significance as it is the only surviving Grand Music Hall in the world. The foremost arts venue in the East End, Wilton's welcomes world-class artistic talent all year round.

Wilton's programmes and produces extraordinary music and theatre, which speak to the magical space of Wilton's and are enhanced by it. It is home to over 300 performances and over 80 productions each year.

Wilton's has been home to the first East End BBC Prom, hosted the London International Mime Festival and championed new writing including plays by James Graham, Patterson Joseph, Chris Thorpe, and Joy Wilkinson. It has hosted international work from Hong Kong to Canada and the team of artistic associates have kept diversity at the heart of all they do.

Recently named the 5th most iconic building in London by *Time Out*, Wilton's has a unique spirit that has captured the imagination of generations of artists for over 160 years. Wilton's invests in the next generation of actors, directors and musicians through its Heritage and Artistic Engagement programmes.

About Bristol Old Vic

Bristol Old Vic is the longest continuously running theatre in the UK and celebrated its 250th anniversary in 2016. The historic playhouse aims to inspire audiences with its own original productions, both at home and on tour, whilst nurturing the next generation of artists, whether that be through their 350-strong Young Company, their many outreach and education projects or their trailblazing artist development programme, Bristol Ferment.

They prioritise their public funding to support experiment and innovation, to allow access to their programme for people who would not otherwise encounter it, or be able to afford it, and to keep their extraordinary heritage alive and animated.

Bristol Old Vic's 2018 redevelopment transformed its front of house into a warm and welcoming space for all of Bristol to enjoy, created a new studio theatre and opened up its unique theatrical heritage to the public for the first time.

Since the March 2020 lockdown, the theatre completely reimagined a digital version of itself; experimented with streamed performances available globally, maintained links with their most vulnerable participants and welcomed live audiences during the moments when restrictions were lifted. Now, once again Bristol Old Vic is thrilled to be able to throw open its doors and welcome back audiences both physically and digitally as it looks towards the future.

A Dead Body in Taos

David Farr is a writer and director. His plays *The Danny Crowe Show*, *Elton John's Glasses*, *Night of the Soul*, *Ramayana*, *The UN Inspector*, *The Heart of Robin Hood*, *The Hunt* and a collection of adaptations have all been published by Faber. He was Artistic Director of London's Gate Theatre from 1995 to 1998, and Joint Artistic Director of Bristol Old Vic from 2002 to 2005. He has directed *Coriolanus* and *Julius Caesar* for the RSC and *The UN Inspector* for the National Theatre. In June 2005 he became Artistic Director of the Lyric Theatre, Hammersmith, where his productions included new versions of *The Odyssey* and Kafka's *Metamorphosis*. In 2009 he became Associate Director of the Royal Shakespeare Company, where his productions of *The Winter's Tale*, *King Lear* and *The Homecoming* opened to critical acclaim. He also writes for television and film, including all six episodes of *The Night Manager* for the BBC, the hit Amazon show *Hanna*, and *The Midwich Cuckoos*, which was released on Sky Max in 2022. He directed the first production of Thomas Adès's *Powder Her Face* for Almeida Opera in 1995. David's first book for children, *The Book of Stolen Dreams*, was published in 2021.

DAVID FARR

A Dead Body in Taos

faber

First published in 2022
by Faber and Faber Limited
74–77 Great Russell Street
London WC1B 3DA

Typeset by Brighton Gray
Printed and bound in the UK by CPI Group (Ltd), Croydon CR0 4YY

A CIP record for this book
is available from the British Library

978-0-571-37970-5

2 4 6 8 10 9 7 5 3 1

Acknowledgements

With thanks to Adam Curtis for his brilliance and inspiration, Kate McGrath for her persistence and vision, and all the actors and artists who workshopped and nurtured the piece on its strange journey.

A Dead Body in Taos was produced by Fuel and co-commissioned by Fuel, Theatre Royal Plymouth and Warwick Arts Centre with support from Bristol Old Vic, and first performed at Bristol Old Vic on 30 September 2022, with the following cast:

Leo David Burnett
Jacob Fellows Nathan Ives-Moiba
Sam Gemma Lawrence
Tristana Cortez/Agnes Martin/Kath's Mum Clara Onyemere
Kath Eve Ponsonby
Curtis Adams/Michael/Dr Fritz Erhardt Dominic Thorburn

All other parts played by members of the company

Director Rachel Bagshaw
Designer Ti Green
Lighting Design Katy Morison
Composition and Sound Design Ben and Max Ringham
Video Design Sarah Readman
Movement Director Ingrid Mackinnon

Accent Coach Gurkiran Kaur
Costume Supervisor Victoria Nissley
Assistant Directors Tian Brown-Sampson,
    Oliwia Charmuszko-Carrigan
Associate Sound Designer Ellie Isherwood
Assistant Costume Supervisor Jo Lewis
Casting Director Louis Hammond CDG
Production Manager Helen Mugridge
Company Stage Manager Roisin Symes

Characters

In Taos
Sam
Taos Police
Leo (older)
Jacob Fellows
Tristana Cortez
Kath Cyborg

In Kath's Past
Kath
Kath's mother
Leo (younger)
Brad
Curtis Adams
Students at Kent State
Agnes Martin
Reporter
Governor Rhodes
Dr Fritz Erhardt
Michael

The play is intended to be performed by six actors or more.

A DEAD BODY IN TAOS

Act One

A dead body found. Police lights in the New Mexican desert. We hear reporter voices, multiple reports.

Reporter Voices The body was found in the hills of the remote New Mexico desert about thirty miles from the small town of Taos at zero-five-hundred hours Pacific Standard Time. The temperatures were twenty below zero and the body frozen cold. The body is reported to be a white female, dressed in light clothing, and to be between sixty and seventy years old.

> *Sam, not actually in the scene, somehow outside but looking in, stares at the body in the police lights.*
> *Sam is thirty-three years old. She has an English accent. Now we are in the mortuary, Taos. Sam is with an American police. Police has a Southern US accent.*

Police Would you like a coffee? Glass of water?

Sam I've just come off a twelve-hour flight. I'd like to get this done and get to the hotel.

Police This won't take long.
  Would you mind confirming? Is this Katherine Horvath?

> *Sam is shown the body.*

Is this your mother?

> *In the distance we see a figure, strange, shadowy, still. It is Kath Cyborg.*
> *Sam looks at the body on the slab.*

Sam Yes, that's her.

Police You came here alone?

Sam Yes. Alone.

Police You are resident in the United Kingdom?

Sam In London. She brought me up there.

Police Could you please write your full address on the form?

Sam How did she die?

Police We're still awaiting a full autopsy.

Sam But . . .

Police (*anticipating her concern*) There was no sign of foul play . . . we can only assume natural causes, from the cold.

Sam Did she get lost?

Police The deceased has lived here many years. She knew the area well. She knew that walking after dark at this time of year would be dangerous. She knew the temperatures . . .

Sam So what are you implying?

Police It's possible she was under the influence. Taos is home to a lot of individuals who maintain habits of various kinds in order to support their alternative view of life.

Sam And if she wasn't under the influence?

Police We must also consider the possibility . . . of a deliberate act.

> *Beat.*

We found a message on your mother's body. It has your name on it.

> *Police hands the message over.*

Do you understand it at all?

> *Sam looks at the message.*
> *In the distance the Kath Cyborg stirs . . .*

14

CREMATION

The coffin of Kath Horvath is behind the curtains. Sam is there in dark clothes. Sam gives the oration. She's not comfortable doing so.

Sam My name is Sam, I'm Kath's only daughter. I'm going to say a few words.

My mother's favourite artist was the abstract expressionist Agnes Martin.

An older man is in the background. Leo. Sixty-five years old. In a dark suit. He watches.

Agnes drew endless grids in pencil. Like she was trying to quieten the world. Make a journey out of chaos.

Pause. Leo watches her.

My mother was obsessed by her, ever since she first saw her work in the mid 1960s. They met back then. Agnes was driving her camper van. My mother was at college. My mother asked Agnes where she was going. She replied, 'Towards the silence.'

When she had her breakdown, my mother chose to come here. Where Agnes Martin died.

She said it was the quietest place on earth.

Sam looks out the window at the mountains as the cremation music plays. Leo watches Sam as the body disappears.

Leo Sam?

My name is Leo Brewer. I'm an old friend of your mother's.

Sam I know who you are.

Leo I flew in from Chicago last night. I wanted to be here.

Sam Chicago?

Leo I teach there now. I was at NYU but they deemed me no longer fit for service. Are you alone?

Sam I'll only be here a few days. I have to get back for work.

Leo Your father didn't want to be here?

Sam I haven't told him she died.

Leo Wouldn't he want to know?

Sam I didn't see the point. He and Kath . . .

Leo You call her Kath?

Sam She hated the word 'mother'. My parents weren't reconciled, as you Americans would say.

Leo Is he still in London?

Sam He's in Switzerland. His second marriage has just failed.

Leo I'm sorry.

Sam Oh he's fine. He lives by his lake counting his money.

Leo It's strange. We never met before.

Sam Why strange? Kath and I haven't been close for a long time.

Leo I haven't seen her in ten years.

Beat.

Sam She talked about you when I was young. She talked about you a lot.

Leo Oh yes?

Sam She was angry with you. For leaving her.

Leo I didn't leave her. She was the love of my life.

They stare at the curtain.

Sam They found a message on her body.

Leo What did it say?

She hands it over. He reads.

'Sam. Don't grieve. I'm not here.'

Sam What does it mean?

Leo stares at the letter.

THE HOUSE

Sam is in her mother's house. She stares out at the horizon. She's on the phone.

Sam I've booked the flight back for Thursday. I need to sort the will, decide what happens with the house. But it shouldn't take long.
    I'm here now. It's like a hermit's cave. You look out the window, there's nothing, just sky and rock.

Beat.

This isn't the time to talk about this.
    Why? Because my mother is dead, I'm in the middle of New Mexico, and now you're suddenly thinking about me?

Jacob Fellows enters. Thirty-five years old. African-American. Briefcase.

The lawyer's here. I have to go. Maybe we can talk about this when we're actually in the same city.
    I'm putting the phone down. Daniel. I'm putting down the phone.

She puts down the phone.

Jacob Miss Felix? Jacob Fellows. I apologise for intruding.

Sam I asked you here.

Jacob Yes you did. I'm sorry for your loss. Kath was a wonderful woman. Full of life. Are you staying here in the house? It's a beautiful place. Did you know that an artist built it?

Sam Agnes Martin.

Jacob Have you been to the gallery in town?

Sam I'm staying at the Angel Falls hotel.

Jacob Oh really? Because just to be clear, it's perfectly permissible for you as her daughter and executor to use the house during this period. Your mother lived alone, there's no one else here . . .

Sam I prefer to use the hotel. Thank you.

Jacob You came to Taos on your own?

Sam Yes, and I need to leave once this is all seen to. I have a life in London. Deadlines. I need to get back.

Beat.

Jacob Are you okay?

Sam Why would I not be okay?

Jacob Well, normally at this time people prefer a little conversation before they get down to the business side. But that's all good.

He opens his briefcase.

Can you confirm that you are Kath Horvath's only living dependant and the executor of her will and testimony?

Sam I can.

Jacob Okay.

He smiles. He opens the letter. He is clearly taken aback.

Okay.

Sam What is it?

Jacob Samantha, may I call you Samantha? May I ask? When did you last speak to your mother?

Sam It was on the phone. Three years ago.

Jacob Did she talk to you? About anything?

Sam She asked me to come here, to Taos. I declined.

Jacob May I ask why?

Sam We hadn't seen each other for a long time. I didn't see any reason to change that.

Jacob Did something happen? I mean, to result in such occasional contact . . .

Sam Is this relevant?

Jacob I don't know. Is it?

Beat.

Miss Felix, your mother's will was changed quite recently. She delivered the new version to my office herself, sealed. Not long before she passed. Wouldn't say what was in it, wouldn't say why. What I am reading here is not what I expected based on our previous conversations.

Beat.

Sam What does it say?

FUTURE LIFE

The Future Life Corporation. Taos. Sam watches a 'welcome' presentation on a screen.

Presenter (*voice-over*) Welcome to Future Life, a research facility situated in the vast beauty of the New Mexican desert. The landscape of Taos and the mountains of the Santa Crista have long been a place of spiritual reflection from the Native Americans through the Catholic invaders to the New Age alternative practices of the twentieth century. Now Future Life biotech corporation builds on these foundations of metaphysical and existential questing to take humanity into the third millennium.

Tristana Cortez is there.

Cortez Miss Felix, I'm sorry, I was delayed in a session. Did someone get you a drink?

Sam What was she doing here?

Cortez I see you have inherited your mother's directness.

Sam That's pretty much all I inherited.

Cortez This must be shocking for you. Please. Can I get you something?
You know the house is yours so long as you choose to stay in it . . .

Sam That's a bequest in the form of a handcuff. I don't want my mother controlling my future or where I live it. I don't even want her money. I do want to know why this institution is her major beneficiary.

Cortez Kath was interested in our work here at FLC. She's always been a seeker. As you know.

Sam And this is where the seekers come to die.

Cortez Not exactly.

Beat.

Sam What do you mean?

Cortez Kath said you'd come. She asked me to show you something. It won't take a minute. And it will explain a great deal about what your mother has been doing these last few years.

Beat.

I'm wondering if maybe you should sit down.

Sam Thank you, I prefer to stand.

Cortez Nonetheless it might be advisable. In our experience . . .

Sam I don't want to sit down.

Beat.

Cortez Jared, would you send Kath through?

Jared (*on intercom*) Certainly, Dr Cortez.

Sam What did you say?

Cortez I really would sit down.

A figure at the door.

Come in, Kath.

Enter a robotic figure. Kath Cyborg. She is around thirty-five years old. She is a cyborg but played by the actress who plays Kath. She has an American accent but speaks without much emotion.

Kath Cyborg Hello, Tristana.

Cortez Hi, Kath. This is Sam.

Kath Cyborg I know who she is.

Beat.

Hello, darling. How are you?

Sam stands astonished, stumbles. Silence.

I was worried you wouldn't come. But here you are. You got my message.

Cortez (*to Sam*) Do you need a glass of water?

Sam I'm fine.

Kath You remember that time I had a party in the house in Belsize Park? It was meant to be fun and you were so nervous you puked up in front of all the guests. You look a little like that now.

Cortez Are you sure you don't need a glass . . .?

Sam I said I'm fine . . .

21

Cortez Kath, do you want to explain to Sam what we're doing here?

Kath Cyborg I think it's better coming from you, Tristana.

Cortez Okay. So five years ago your mother signed on to the FLC Life After Death programme. In so doing she offered her story and all intellectual property associated to Future Life Corporation. And our work here began.

Kath Cyborg I came here every day. I told Tristana everything. Everything I experienced in my life, every moment I remembered. Every feeling. Every memory.

Cortez It was some effort. Your mother had therapy, as you know, all her life, many kinds, so she was highly skilled at emotional and biographical recall. The rest she left to myself and the AI programmers.

Beat.

Jared, can we have that glass of water in here please?

Sam Why does she look like that?

Kath Cyborg That was my choice.

Cortez The physical representation is from May 1986.

Kath Cyborg The year I had you.

Cortez It's based on photographic material and archival VHS from which our 3D modellers were able to create the simulacrum you see before you. Height and weight are precise, facial detailing we're still working on. The voice lacks a certain emotional range. We'll improve that over time.

Kath Cyborg But listen. None of that matters, Sam. What matters is that I'm your mother.

For a moment Sam walks towards Kath Cyborg. Then turns.

Sam (*to Cortez, about to leave*) Dr Cortez, thank you.

Cortez Ms Felix. I know it's a lot to take on.

Sam I'll need to research the legal position on this.

Kath Cyborg Darling, please don't lawyer up without a conversation.

Sam (*to Cortez*) Can I ask one thing? Was this your idea? Did you prey on her vanity? Seduce her into coming here?

Kath Cyborg She didn't force me to do anything, darling. I came to her. I was of sound mind. I still am.

Sam Please don't call me darling. I am not your darling.
   I have to return to London. There are only three of us at the art magazine where I work, and I said I wouldn't be away long. I will therefore put this in the hands of lawyers who will see to it that the will is contested . . .

   Sam lights a cigarette. Her hand shakes.

Cortez Miss Felix, please pause a moment. Your mother left you a message in her coat pocket because she wanted to give you a choice. Of course you can leave here, contest the will and you may win.

Kath Cyborg Though they do have experience in that area.

Cortez But say you do. In that case there would be no funds available to continue your mother's experiment here at Future Life and we would have to close her programme down. Five years of work will be destroyed. The entire physical representation. All the AI data and algorithms. We will wipe her out. Or more correctly, you will. And then she really will be dead.
   So before you do that, please listen to her. Delay your flight back. Stay at the house. Spend time with Kath. Listen to her side.

   Beat.

Sam No. It's too late.

Kath Cyborg Sam. Please don't leave me.
Give me one more chance.
Please.

Sam looks at Kath Cyborg.

CAKE MIX

TV (*voice-over*) And then, ladies, add the egg. Do that now.

A Midwest US town, 1968. A mother, forty-five years old, is baking at her kitchen. The TV is on.

Because this cake mix needs that special touch that only a loving housewife can give it . . .

She adds the egg.

Betty Crocker's cake mix is now ready to pop in the oven . . .

The phone rings. On the phone is Kath Horvath. She is seventeen years old. Both have American accents.

Kath Hi, Mom.

Mother Katherine, is that you? Where are you? Dinner's already on.

Kath I'm not going to have dinner tonight, Mom.

Mother What do you mean?

Kath I'm at the bus station.

Mother What you doing at the bus station, dear?

Kath Come on, Mom. You know. It's been coming for a while.

Mother It's raining out there, honey. You haven't even got your raincoat. It's on the hook in the hall.

Kath I'm leaving.

Beat.

Mother Where are you going?

Kath I think I'm going to the city. Maybe I'll enrol in college there.

Mother To do what?

Kath I don't know. Maybe paint or something.

Mother How can you enrol in / college?

Kath I don't know, Mom, / I'll find a way.

Mother You didn't even finish your schooling.

Kath I don't know! Okay.

Mother Let me get your father.

Kath No, don't get him. I don't want to talk to him.

Mother Listen, you know your father . . . he's ice and fire.

Kath Don't fetch him, Mom. We're done here.

Beat.

Mother What do I do with your room?

Kath I don't know.

Mother I'll keep it. I'll keep it the same. One day you might want to come back. One day . . .

Kath I have to go.

Mother At least let me bring your raincoat.

Kath The bus is leaving, Mom. Say goodbye to Billy for me.

Mother Kath. Write to me. Give me a number I can call you on. Don't disappear, Kath. Please don't disappear.

Kath hangs up and runs for her bus.
Music – Bob Dylan's 'I Want You'.

Leo I'm not supporting the Vietcong! I am simply saying that . . .

Brad You're a fucking peacenik, man!

Kent State University, 1968. Two students in the common room. Arguing. One is young Leo. He is nineteen years old.

Leo And what does your warmongering achieve, Brad? First Vietnam. Next Cambodia? Where else?

Brad I got friends out in Vietnam. My father lost a leg at Pearl Harbor. Don't tell me what war does not achieve.

Kath enters, eighteen years old. She looks dirty, tired. She has her bag over her shoulder. She sees Leo.

Leo So you're not going to sign?

Brad No I'm not. You wave that thing in front of my face again I'll ram it down your fucking throat.

He leaves.

Leo (*shouting after him*) Point taken!

Beat. He sees Kath.

Well you can't win them all.

Kath I guess.

Leo Have we met? I'm Leo. Leo Brewer.

Kath Kath Horvath. No we haven't.

Leo Are you interested in signing?

Kath Signing what?

Leo It's to demand the university divest from all funding from government and state bodies until the US withdraws from Vietnam.

Kath Sure. I'll sign that.

Leo If only everyone was that easy.

Kath Oh I'm not easy.

She signs.

Leo I've not seen you around.

Kath Just got here. I enrolled late.

Leo What are you studying?

Kath Art.

Leo I'm majoring in politics. Minor in psychology.

Kath So you're going to bore me shitless and read my mind.

Leo Something like that.

Kath You're Jewish?

Leo Can you tell?

Kath Everyone used to think I was Jewish at home cos my name's Horvath. But I'm not. Just plain old Lutheran.

Leo Home being . . .

Kath Iowa.

Leo New York.

Kath Oh wow.

Leo Well, New Jersey technically. So why Kent State?

Kath They took me. Someone had to, I guess.

Leo You okay? You look like you haven't eaten in days.

Kath I left home six weeks ago. I been spending every night sleeping in bus stations in Cleveland. I don't really know where I am.
    Is there some water? I feel a little dizzy.

Leo Sure.

She starts to have a panic attack.

Hey. It's okay. It's okay. Breathe. Breathe. I'll call someone. The college has medical staff.

Kath No, don't call any staff.
   I don't have any money. I don't have anyone. I faked my grades and my financial information to get in here.

Leo Listen, maybe we should call your mum and dad.

Kath No. Never. NEVER AGAIN. You hear?

Leo Okay. I hear.

Kath Hold me. I feel like I'm bursting apart.

He holds her. She grasps him.

Don't let me go.

Leo I won't.

Kath Don't let me go.

Kath holds on to Leo for her life.
Music – Jimi Hendrix's 'The Wind Cries Mary'.

UNDUE INFLUENCE

Sam and Jacob are at the house. The windows look out on to the desert.

Jacob You asked me to look into the grounds for challenging your mother's will.

Sam Yes.

Jacob Which I have done. Your mother paid Future Life a total of one million seven hundred thousand dollars over the last five years. And the ongoing contract exists at nearly five hundred thousand dollars a year.

Sam It's not about the money. I want to make that clear. The money I will throw in the desert just like I did her ashes.

Jacob It's not my business what you do with the money . . .

Sam I just want to close the programme down.

Jacob My investigations lead me to believe you have a case. Undue Influence.

Sam What is that?

Jacob Undue Influence is cited where it is claimed the deceased was unethically influenced by a person or group of persons prior to their death. In this case, with such a late change of testament, and with an organisation as enigmatic as Future Life, I believe there is every chance we could argue this in your favour.

Sam I assume you don't need me to be here while that proceeds? I have a flight leaving tomorrow.

Jacob It's not quite as simple as that. If we are to challenge the will, your relationship with your mother will come under the microscope. We will need to show that the estrangement between you was caused by her own actions which she later regretted. They are bound to ask what happened between the two of you. They will want to open . . . old wounds. Why you didn't speak for so long.

Sam And if I don't wish to say?

Jacob It may weaken your case. Which is why if there is something in your history that could be a problem for us, I would prefer to know it now.

Beat.

Sam No avoiding it.

Jacob I'm sorry.

Sam I'm going to have a glass of wine. Will you join me?

Jacob I probably shouldn't . . .

Sam One glass, Mr Attorney. Open it, would you?

She holds out the bottle.

EXPRESSION

Leo I like it.

Kath Yeah?

Kent State University, 1969. Kath makes art. Freedom murals. Pop-art style.

Leo You can really paint. No wonder you're getting top grades.

Kath I used to make murals on the walls in my dad's garage, but one Sunday he spray-painted over them all.

Leo He did what?

Kath Said they were un-American. You'd have to meet my dad to understand. On second thoughts don't. It wouldn't end well.

Leo What's un-American is not allowing a person to express themselves. First goddamn Amendment.

Kath Well that's not such a big thing in the garages of Iowa. You want to add something into this?

Leo Me? Into your painting?

Kath Why not introduce the arbitrary?

Leo I'm not a very arbitrary person.

Kath Well maybe that should change.

She holds out the brush. He takes it. Hesitates.

You afraid to express yourself, Leo?

She smiles.

Leo I can't. It's your work.

Kath Fucking prude. Express yourself. DO IT!

He does so. Sudden frenzy. Then he stops. Looks at his work.

Leo Oh my God. What have I done?

Kath You've expressed yourself.

Leo I've destroyed your painting. I'm a vandal.

Kath It is kind of awful.

Leo I should be locked up.

Kath Leo, relax.

Leo How can you not care? I desecrated your work.

Kath So I'll paint another one. It's only Monday.

Leo I think that makes you a genius.

Kath I think that makes you very sweet.

They look at each other.

Leo I should go. I have a class.

Beat.

Kath Leo. Before you go. Can I express something to you?

Leo I guess.

She kisses him.

Okay.

Kath Okay what?

Leo Okay I want to do that again.

Kath All right. But listen. Once we kiss again, I'm yours forever. You understand that?

Leo Forever? Like in some fairy tale?

Kath Exactly like that. So it's your choice . . . because when these lips touch . . .

He kisses her.
Leo and Kath make love in her room.

SEPARATION

The house in Taos.
Later. The bottle of wine is almost empty. Sam has drunk most of it. She is in her memories.

Sam The truth is she should never have been with him.

Jacob With your father?

Sam Who else? He made her live in a house in the Surrey green belt. Lawnmowers and golf clubs, of which he was of course a member. It was everything she hated.

Jacob So they separated.

Sam When I was fifteen.

Jacob Was there infidelity involved?

Sam Both sides. A court case, over money, over me. Which my mother won.

Beat.

And then, only once she'd won, did she tell me . . .
She said she couldn't look after me on her own. She said that my issues . . .

Jacob Issues?

Sam I was a teenager in an overly rich, insufficiently interesting small town. I drank too much. I took ecstasy at the weekend – who didn't?

Jacob Probably me.

Sam Kath put me into a boarding school. I lasted less than a year. My father came to fetch me. Suddenly the exclusion orders and custody battle seemed to mean nothing to her. She couldn't have been happier to see me go.

Jacob So she was at that time an unsatisfactory parent.

Sam My father got me through school, he treated it like the completion of some contract, a series of legal obligations. But he had another family by then. Two more children.

Jacob You didn't feel part of the family.

Sam Which is why when my mother came back into my life . . . much later . . .

Jacob It meant a great deal to you.

Sam Are you practising for the courtroom?

Jacob It's my job.

Beat.

Sam I was a mess, I'd had a series of relationships. One abusive.
She came and rescued me, took me to her place in Dorset, this was her organic farming phase . . . I stayed with her for a while. I was studying art history at the time, or trying to.

Jacob The bond was re-established.

Sam She even cooked for me, It was the only time. Not for long, just a few weeks. Like she was trying to love me. But then . . . I could feel it. Something got in the way. Some rage. Or pride. Like she was so intent on her own integrity, she couldn't let anyone else in. She began to resent me. One night we had a fight. A real fight.

Jacob Who started it?

Sam Does it matter?

33

Jacob It matters.

Sam She threw the first stone. It was a toaster but you get the idea.

Jacob She started the fight.

Sam I gave as good as I got. She bled. I fractured a wrist. I left. Went to London.
 The court might refer to it as a dark period.
 Then I get an email. Saying that she loves me but she can't leap the barriers. She's having a breakdown of some kind. She's leaving to come here to Taos. I will always be her girl. All her money she will leave to me.

Jacob All her money? You have the email?

Sam I deleted it instantly.

Jacob But she wrote it. In which case it might be on her server.

Sam We didn't speak for seven years. Then she got in contact. Asked me to come here. I declined.

 Beat. She drinks fast.

Jacob Did she ever say why she wanted you to come? Did she ever mention Future Life?

Sam No.

Jacob So you had no idea that she was in the arms of this organisation that was turning her brain and angling after her money.

Sam No, Mr Attorney, I had no idea.

Jacob Are you all right?

Sam I feel strange.

Jacob Maybe you should go slow on the wine.

Sam Maybe we should open another bottle.

Jacob I think that would not be wise.

Sam You sound like my father talking to my mother.

Jacob We can leave it there for tonight. I should probably get back.

Sam Killjoy.

Jacob I have an early start.

Sam Is Mrs Fellows waiting for you?

Jacob Nothing like that.

Sam I assumed. The ring.

Jacob You assumed wrong.
I'll let you know how I get on.

Sam Don't go yet. Please. I feel very alone here.

He withdraws.

Jacob Miss Felix. That would not be wise.

Sam I'm sorry.

Jacob That's quite all right.

Sam Are you okay to drive?

Jacob I know the road well. And I only had a glass.

He leaves. Sam continues to drink the wine.

LOUDER

Curtis 'I am more and more convinced that man is a selfish, brutal, bestial animal controlled only by fear and desire.'

1968. Professor Curtis Adams, forty years old, professor of philosophy and politics, is giving a symposium at Kent State University to a group of eager students, Kath and Leo among them. Kath smokes.

'Man's sadistic impulses, his ferocious appetite, his rage and jealousy, will in the coming years be unleashed in its full horror. Whoever can connect with and manipulate these forces, of fear and desire, will be master of us all.'

Sigmund Freud wrote that in 1917. In so doing, he predicted the twentieth century.

Leo Freud was talking about German nationalism.

Curtis Of course he was. But he was also talking about us. About America.

Student McCarthy witch-hunts.

Student Corporate control of the mind.

Curtis The battle over who we are. Are we just animals governed by passion? Or can we think for ourselves? What about you, Kath? You think you're free?

Kath Sure I'm free.

Curtis Okay, so for example. Why do you smoke?

Kath Because it's fucking great.

She exhales.

Curtis Why did you start?

Kath Because my dad hated it.

Curtis Rebellion. You wanted to feel free. Right?

Kath Damn right.

Curtis In 1927 a New York publicist persuaded the women of New York to smart smoking. You know how? He got twelve of the most beautiful West College girls to light up on 42nd Street. And he invited half the press of New York there to watch them. He said the girls were lighting torches of freedom. The papers sucked it up and it worked. Suddenly women started smoking for liberty. And you're still doing it today. The Statue of Nicotine.

Kath Now I'm quitting.

Curtis You're addicted. Too late.

Leo So what then? If our government and our corporations are using us, the way you say, then what? What do we do?

Curtis Well that's what I teach.

Leo Yeah but beyond teaching. Beyond getting a fucking degree. No one changed the world with a diploma.

Curtis Well thank you, Leo. Then protest. Form collectives. Make your voice heard. Free your minds.

Leo Professor.

Curtis Call me Curtis. Please.

Leo Curtis. Campuses have been full of protest, full of banners, and it makes no difference. Governments don't listen to students. It's just pointless noise. It's like screaming in a wind tunnel. No one hears.

Curtis So be louder.

> *Kath stares at him. Smiles. Music. Richie Havens's 'Handsome Johnny'.*
> *Kath makes protest paintings against the war. On the walls.*
> *Leo is reading.*

Leo I'm trying to read!

Kath What?

Leo I said I'm trying to read!

Kath What? WHAT? WHAT?

> *She smiles, turns the music up.*

He said be louder, Leo.

Leo Fuck you, but I love you.

Kath I LOVE YOU.

They dance to the music.
On the screens, student demonstrations. Protests.
She paints, dances. Leo watches. A little scared.

HAPPY IN ILLINOIS

Future Life. Kath Cyborg and Sam.

Kath Cyborg I heard you delayed your flight back.

Sam Just while we sort the legal case. Then I have to go. I have so much work.

Kath Cyborg At the 'art magazine'.

Sam Why do you say it like that?

Kath Cyborg Why are you here today? If all you're interested in is 'the legal case' . . .

Sam I was hoping you'd agree to stop this.

Kath Cyborg I'm a machine, my dear. I can't make that decision.

Sam If you're who you claim to be, you absolutely can.

   Beat.

Kath Cyborg What did you do with my ashes?

Sam I scattered them in the hills outside the house.

Kath Cyborg Without my permission?

Sam I didn't know what to do with them. I wasn't going to take them back with me on the plane.

Kath Cyborg It's very presumptuous of you to throw my ashes when I'm not even dead.
   Did you do it alone?

Sam No. With Leo Brewer.

Kath Cyborg With Leo?

Sam Yes. He came to the funeral. Flew in from Chicago.

Kath Cyborg Did you talk to him?

Sam Of course. I liked him.

Kath Cyborg He's back with his partner in Chicago now.

Sam Yes, he said.

Kath Cyborg Did he tell you about her?

Sam Yes, Mum, he did. They seem happy.

Kath Cyborg Happy. That's a great destination for one of life's political revolutionaries. Happy in Illinois. Did he cry at my cremation?

Sam Oh for God's sake.

Kath Cyborg I'm interested.

Sam No he didn't cry. He wore a dark suit. He offered his consolations and then he got back on the plane. Tell them to stop this. Please. It's futile.

Kath Cyborg I was hoping you were enjoying this conversation.

Sam It's not a conversation. You're impersonating my mother. I listen. Out of duty. But you're not my mother. You're an algorithm.

Kath Cyborg In my human form what was I? A bunch of cell structures. Neurons transmitting nerve information through synapses, hundreds of thousands of chemical reactions. What am I now? What's the difference? Only that you can't touch me and feel my warmth. That I understand. But otherwise . . .

Sam There are things you can't know . . . feelings, nuances . . .

Kath Cyborg Only if I've forgotten. In which case what's the difference?

Sam Of course there's a difference. There'll be memories, impressions, fears, that are deep inside. So that the person I'm talking to now, cannot be the Kath I knew.

Kath Cyborg Remember my hairdresser in Camden?

Sam Yes of course. Gwendoline . . .

Kath Cyborg Ah, she was something. Three lovers. Weekday Man, Weekend Charlie and, whenever he flew in, Jamaican Gary. I liked Gwendoline. You liked her too, I think. You'd come and watch me have my hair done, down that grimy little alleyway. I got her to wash your hair once. You remember? You loved the feeling of her hands massaging your scalp. You said it was so tender.

Beat.

Sam (*sudden emotion*) Mum, I don't want to pursue this legal case. I just want to live my life again. Tell them it's over. Please.

Kath Cyborg Why do you think I chose this form, Sam? Why did you think I wanted you here? I failed you as a mother. Of all the failures of my life, you were the greatest.

Sam Well that makes me feel better.

Kath Cyborg I was so unhappy when I left London for America. I felt spiritually shattered. When I met Dr Cortez, she asked me the reason for my unhappiness. I told her my relationships had failed. I had an estranged husband, a daughter in London who hated me, who didn't want to talk to me, whom I had lost, through my own doing. When she explained what they were doing here I saw a chance, to recreate myself, as a better person. Here in Taos. At great personal cost. I looked into my soul. Confessed. I did it for you.

Sam Why can't you just let me go?

Kath Cyborg I'm a fighter. Always was.

FIRE

Kent State University, 1970.
    Curtis and Kath have just made love.

Kath He's such a coward. I swear to God every time I talk about positive action, he goes pale. Back to his petitions and committee meetings.

Curtis Leo's middle class. He doesn't have your fearlessness.

Kath Yeah well, I'm getting tired of it. I switched courses for him. I gave up art.

Curtis For him?

Kath You think I did it for you?

Curtis I thought you did it for yourself.

Kath No, you thought I did it for you. To be taught by the great master.
    I feel so dirty.

Curtis For switching classes, or . . .?

Kath Don't tell him we did this. It would kill his bourgeois East Coast soul. He'd try so hard to understand my reasons for fucking you I think he might have a stroke.

Curtis What were your reasons?

Kath Well the opportunity was gaping.

41

Curtis Is that all?

Kath And you got me high.

Curtis You got yourself high, Kath. You're a free woman.

Kath No woman is free.

Curtis Women have never been more empowered. The feminist movement is driving the agenda.

Kath And middle-aged men like you support it with all your fucking hearts.

She laughs. Then stops.

I fucked you because I was furious.

Curtis At who?

Kath I don't know.

Curtis It's dangerous, that anger of yours. It's like a flame that needs telling what to burn. I've seen you at the meetings. It's powerful, you've got a big following now. People connect to you. But it's kind of reckless. Needing to break every rule.

Kath I thought you liked that.

Curtis Where does it come from?

Kath All my own, buddy.

Curtis Passion like that. There's always a source.

Kath Is there, Professor?

Curtis Your father ever visited you here?

Kath Oh come on. You serious?

Curtis Has he?

Kath Are you trying to psychoanalyse me twenty minutes after fucking me?

Curtis I'm asking you a question.

Kath My father's not here because I didn't invite him. Because I don't want his ugly face anywhere near me or my studies. Although. I did think about him when I was screwing you. Do you think that's a problem, Professor?

She grins wickedly.

Curtis You can't change anything if you don't know yourself. You're bringing a university campus to boiling point with a rage that you don't even begin to understand.

Kath You're scared of me.

Curtis Only because you're playing with fire.

Kath Professor Adams. I am fire.

Music. West Coast Pop Art Experimental Band's 'Suppose They Give A War (And No One Comes)'.
The campus grounds. Kent State.
Kath and Leo hold the Constitution. Kath speaks with passion.

This is a protest against our government and against our university that refuses to voice its opposition to the war in Vietnam.

But more than that. This is a protest against America. The America that says, 'We will buy whatever you want us to buy because it will make us feel better, make us desire ourselves more, make us feel good.' The America that says, 'We will support whatever war you want us to support, we will follow the leaders you want us to follow, not because we've decided that's best for us. But because our terrors drive us into your arms.' This is the manufacture of consent. And we're living it. Every day in the United States of America. But we say no. We are not happiness machines! We are human beings!

So rise up and raise your voices. In anger. In rage. Bury the Constitution with us. Together we can change this college, this country. We can change the world!

Kath buries the Constitution.
 The crowd roars.
 Music rises. Kath salutes. Leo smiles. She kisses him.

Hold me.

Leo What's wrong?

Kath I feel I could explode right open. Hold me, Leo. Hold me tight.

THE NEXT LEVEL

Future Life. Cortez and Sam.

Cortez I want to explain why you're so important to what we're doing here.

 Beat.

Your mother has given me a unique opportunity. The chance to take the human mind somewhere it has never been. Into a whole new form. To do that I need to look at what she knows. But also what she does not know. What she thinks she knows but does not. What she thinks she does not know but actually knew all along. To create the false hopes, the self-delusion, the layers of deception inherent in every human action. Everyone thinks it's our brilliance, our speed, our complexity that's hard to mimic. You know what's hard? The mess is what's hard. The inefficiency. The fact that you're now thinking as much about what I'm thinking about you, about your mother, and you're making assumptions, about my motives, my intentions, that are almost all wrong, but the fact you're doing it is what makes you, you. And the fact that your mother, being your mother, does it with more aggression and more blind rage than anyone I've ever met, makes her the most perfect challenge of all. In my field we call this the conscious paradox. How do you create a person who has

44

no idea who they are? I'll tell you one way. You need the people she loves.

Sam And by that you mean me?

Cortez I've seen you with your mother. I know there's a connection forming. Not just for her. But for you too. It's real. And it's changing both of you. Love is the most complex of all our operating mechanisms. But it's the one that fascinates me the most.

Stay here. Live in your mother's house. Work with me. And your mother.

Isn't that what you really want?

SILENCE

1970. Agnes Martin and Kath meet in front of a camper van on the Kent State campus.

Kath Excuse me.
Can I help you?

Agnes I'll be on my way soon.

Kath Is this your van?

Agnes Sure.

Kath I'm Kath.

Agnes My name is Agnes.

Kath What do you do, Agnes?

Agnes I paint. At least I used to. Now mostly I just drive.

Kath Drive where?

Agnes I've been driving across America.

Kath How long for?

Agnes I suppose it must be . . . two years.

Kath You have any paintings with you?

Agnes Oh no, I left all that behind.

Beat.

Kath I know who you are. You're Agnes Martin. I studied you. I love your work.

Agnes You study painting?

Kath I gave up. Switched to politics.

Agnes Then I guess paint wasn't for you.
What was all the noise on the field?

Kath We buried the Constitution. As a protest.

Agnes Against what?

Kath Everything. You want to join us? We're going to demonstrate in the town, the campus, we're tearing it up here.

Agnes I think I'll move on.

Kath What are you looking for? When you paint?

Agnes I'm looking for silence.

Kath Me too. But I can't paint here. Things are too noisy.

Agnes And they're going to get noisier.

OHIO

In Taos, Sam is drinking. Bottle of wine. From the bottle.

Sam I've delayed my flight. I just have to. I have to finish this. Because I thought I buried her. But I haven't.
You won't believe me, Daniel. But my mother is still alive. In fact she's more alive than ever.

Music – Neil Young's 'Ohio'.
News footage.

46

Kath and Leo amongst it. Banners.
Beat.

Reporter The violence escalated at Kent State University this weekend. On Saturday the campus was in lockdown as the RITC building was burnt to the ground and the National Guard moved in to calm tensions. Governor James A. Rhodes was kept informed as a stand-off ensued that spread into Sunday May fourth. Governor Rhodes, who is currently running for senator, visited the campus on Sunday morning.

Governor Rhodes These people who just move from one campus to another terrorising our community are worse than the brownshirts, worse than the communist element, the night riders and vigilantes, they're the worse type of people we harbour in America. And I want to say this. We will take all necessary action to deal with them.

Kath and Leo line up against the Guardsmen. Kath throws stones.

Reporter By Monday morning a large crowd gathered on the Commons, protesting against the war, the Governor and against President Richard Nixon. The assembly was blocked by Guardsmen. They were ordered to disperse. When the students refused, tear gas was released. Some students picked up the gas and threw it back. Black flags were waved. Anti-Vietnam slogans were shouted. Then something went wrong. As the Guardsmen moved across Blanket Hill to disperse the crowd, bullets were fired, initially into the air. Students fled towards the parking lot. A few rocks were thrown. Then a small group of Guardsmen fired bullets into the crowd. As the crowd fled in terror, students fell, wounded. Four people died.

Kath and Leo watch it happen.

Jeffrey Miller died instantly after being shot in the mouth. He was twenty-one.

Allison Krause, aged nineteen, was shot in the chest and died later that day.

William Schroeder, nineteen years old, was shot in the chest and died later that day.

Sandra Lee Scheuer was walking by chance on her way to her accommodation block and was shot in the neck. She died later that day.

Kath and Leo watch it happen.
At Future Life, Sam, drunk, bursts into the room where the cyborg is waiting. Cortez follows.

Cortez Sam, please come out of the room.

Sam Show me your real face.

Kath Cyborg Sam my dear, calm down.

Sam You do not tell me to calm down. You are not my mother!

Kath Cyborg You're drunk. This is not going to achieve anything.

Sam rips the face off the cyborg.

Cortez Miss Felix. That thing is just the shell. It's not her. I can just build another one.

Sam attacks the Kath Cyborg and destroys it.

Kath Cyborg What are you doing, darling?

Sam You are not my mother! My mother is dead.

Kath Cyborg What are you doing, darling?

Sam My mother is dead! My mother is dead!

Sam rips up the cyborg taking the face off, destroying the inner workings. Kath's voice slows and distorts.

Kath Cyborg What are you doing, darling? What are you doing?

Sam stands there with the destroyed cyborg in her hands.

Act Two

The House in Taos. Jacob and Sam.

Jacob Are you okay?

Sam Yeah.

Jacob You shouldn't have gone there.

Sam I know.

Jacob It renders us vulnerable to a counter-claim . . .

Sam I know, Jacob. I'm not an idiot.

Jacob In which case please refrain from visiting in the future.

Sam Message received.

> *Beat.*

Jacob While I'm here I'd like to look on your mother's computer for that email she wrote to you back in 2010. As her executor's representative I have the right to look through all her correspondence but I wanted to check . . .

Sam It's fine by me.

Jacob You go to bed now. I'll let myself out.

Sam Thank you for coming to pick me up.

Jacob No problem.

> *He opens the computer, starts to work.*

Sam Jacob.

Jacob Yes.

Sam The ring on your finger.

Jacob I *was* married. For a while.

Sam She left?

Jacob I suppose she did, in a way. A car accident out on Route 65.

Beat.

Some drunk kid. Head-on.

Sam When?

Jacob Six years ago.

Sam That must make this whole thing . . .

Jacob I don't know what that makes this. And I apologise if by telling you I am contravening the professional client relationship. But I do feel I have some conception of what you are going through.

Sam How old was she?

Jacob Twenty-eight.

Beat.

Sam What do you think my mother is trying to do in there?

Jacob I think she is trying to delay the inevitable.

Sam Isn't that understandable?

Jacob I'm a Reformed Presbyterian, Miss Felix. I don't find death an obstacle to be avoided. But a gateway to be celebrated.

Sam I don't believe – in anything. When I looked at her dead body on the slab, all I saw was skin and bone. But now. I talk to that machine they've made in there. It's not her. I know it's not. But it is . . .

Jacob It's consoling. Like a memory.

Sam Maybe a memory of something we never had. Or maybe it's a healing.

Jacob Well. There's no immediate rush to make a decision. You've changed your flight. You have time. It's the most important thing with grief.

Sam This is going to sound crazy. But I don't want to hurt her.

Jacob You couldn't hurt her if you tried.

THE TIBETAN CUSHION

Kent State, 1970. Kath in their room. Kath lights a cigarette. Leo enters. She is quiet. She barely speaks above a murmur.

Leo Sandra's parents are here. They're fetching her stuff.

Kath Uh-huh.

Leo Is that all you're going to say?

Kath What do you want me to say?

Leo Maybe you want to meet them? Maybe you want to express some regret?

Kath You want me to say I regret doing what we did?

Leo Our classmate died. She wasn't even part of the demonstration. Can we have a moment of feeling for that?

Kath I didn't shoot her.

Leo It was our protest. We organised it. You and me.

Kath The National Guard gunned down four of our own students.

Leo And I feel responsible.

Kath I don't.

Leo Wow. You are cold as ice.

Kath You're a coward.

Leo My friend just died.

Kath Freedom costs.

Beat.

What do you see when you look in the mirror? I'll tell you
what I see.

She studies herself.

I see a tissue of lies that need unlearning. A heap of shit that
my parents, my high school, my college, my friends, and
you, dear sweet Leo, plugged in there for your own
purposes. Yeah you did. You wanted to go to bed with me,
so you made me sign your petition, join your protest group,
got me into politics. Then when I got more engaged than
you, you tried to buy into my radicalism because it made
you feel good. But the reality is it scared you. Because at
heart you're the son of good New Jersey folk. You're an
obedient little worker, a dog at a bone, all your life, and you
always will be, until you realise it's not your bone. Someone
threw you the bone, and they'll keep throwing it cos you'll
keep gnawing.

Leo How can you say any of that on a day like today?

Kath Maybe you just don't want to know who I really am.

Leo Maybe I don't.

Kath You don't want me? I'll leave.
Do you want me to leave, Leo?

Leo No. Of course not.

Kath Do you still love me?

She looks at him. Beat.

Okay, that's my answer.

Leo No, wait. Where are you going?

Kath I'm leaving the university.

Leo What? Because I paused? Because I thought about whether I love you?

Kath Yes. Because you paused. I do not pause when it comes to love.

Leo What about your course?

Kath Fuck the course. I only did it for you.

She gets up.

Leo No, Kath, wait. Where will you go?

Kath What do you care?
Oh by the way. I slept with Curtis Adams.

Beat.

Leo You're just saying that.

Kath Ask the man himself. I'm sure he'll give you an honest answer.

Music – Buffalo Springfield's 'For What It's Worth'.
Dr Fritz Erhardt. Esalen Institute of Human
Improvement. California, 1970.

Erhardt Okay, welcome, everyone, to today's session. Today we'll be working with someone who's been with the Institute for just a few weeks. Kath, please come forward.

Enter Kath. In 'soft clothes'.

This is Kath. Kath, you arrived at Esalen, when?

Kath Three months ago.

Erhardt You left your campus at Kent State shortly after the shootings there. You took a Greyhound bus west, am I right?

Kath Yeah, I just needed to get out.

Erhardt You were one of the demonstration organisers? You felt responsible.

Kath I don't know what I felt. I knew one of the victims, from class, and my then boyfriend and I kind of . . . fell out. So it wasn't an amenable situation any more.

Erhardt And on the bus you met a young man named Todd. Todd, are you here?

Todd Yeah I'm here. Hi, Kath.

Kath Hi, Todd.

Erhardt Okay, and Todd had been on our transcendental meditation course here and one thing led to another . . . Okay. But Kath has not been finding it easy here. In fact she's thinking of leaving. Can you explain why, Kath?

Kath I don't know if I can.

Erhardt Why are you being so shy? Tell us the problem you have with us all here.

Kath I don't want to be offensive.

Erhardt Be offensive.

Kath You just seem really up your mystic West Coast asses, you know?

Erhardt Why?

Kath Look, I know this is meant to be a rejection of all of the whole American capitalist vortex that we find ourselves in. I know that and I dig it to some extent. But people are dying out there in Vietnam, dying in Kent State where I come from. Really dying and you looking into your psyche for hours and hours, I don't know if that's helping anyone.

Erhardt And it pisses you off . . .

Kath Yeah it kind of does . . .

Erhardt How much?

Kath What do you mean?

Erhardt I want to see how much it pisses you off.

Kath You want me to draw it? I can draw. That's my thing.

Erhardt No, I don't want you to draw it. I want to see it. I don't think you're being honest with me, Kath. I WANT TO SEE YOUR ANGER.

Kath What do you mean?

Erhardt Come on, don't lie to me, bitch. I want to see it.

Kath What did you call me?

Erhardt You heard me.

Kath You want to see it, asshole?

Erhardt Yeah I want to see it. Come on. Take this bag and show me . . .

Kath All right.

Erhardt This bag is my face.

Kath Okay.

She smashes the bag.

There you go. How's that?

Erhardt Is that all? Fucking hundreds dying every day, we're lolling on our hippy asses here, and that's all you got to say?

Kath No, that's not all I got to say, but punching some fucking Tibetan cushion isn't going to do it!

Erhardt All right. So hit me.

Kath What did you say?

Erhardt Go on, hit me.

Kath Well since you asked.

Kath slaps him hard.

Erhardt Good. Now go further. Cos it's not just me, is it? It's just not here either. It's everywhere you fucking go. Lies and bullshit. Right? So what you going to do?

Kath I don't fucking know!

Erhardt Go on!! Take that energy. Bust out of it. Come on!

He grabs her.

Kath Get off me.

Erhardt Come on! You're stronger than that. Bust out of this vice-like grip I got you in. Tell me how it feels!

Kath Get the hell off me!

Kath howls. Tears him off her.

Erhardt Good! Go on! Find it!

Kath tears at herself.

That's good. Rip it all off! Howl! Tear your clothes! Turn the lights off! Turn the lights off, you bunch of peepshow creeps!

Darkness. Kath tears at her clothes, howls, screams.

Go on. No one's watching. Let it go. You can do it. Let it all go. What can you see?

Kath Blackness.

Erhardt No. Bullshit. That's bullshit! You can see something! What can you see?

Kath I see my mother. Bitch.

Erhardt Good! What's she doing?

Kath She's making a cake. She's got Betty Crocker cake mix. She's putting an egg in the cake mix. Like they tell you to on the cardboard box.

Erhardt You know why they put that on the box? Just add an egg?

Kath To make her feel like a good little housewife.

Erhardt That's right. To make her feel that she's contributing to the society we live in by adding one egg to her mix. What do you want to do to that cake mix?

Kath I want to piss in the cake mix.

Erhardt Go on. Piss in it. Piss in it.

She pisses.

Kath I want to take a shit in the cake mix.

Erhardt Go on. Take it. That's good. All those cake mixes that all those women like your bitch cunt mother had to make in their perfect kitchens in their perfect Midwest houses, they're all in your power now. No one can tell you the recipe. You're naked, you're covered in your own filth like the day you were born. Cry, baby. Cry.

Kath cries like a baby.

Okay. Now you're empty. Now you're free.

THE POST

Future Life. Sam and Kath Cyborg.

Kath Cyborg Tell me about the post you issued three months ago. On Facebook. Monday twenty-third January at oh-one-forty-one.

Sam How do you know about that?

57

Kath Cyborg The researchers needed all the information they could garner so they found a way to become your friend . . . a touch unethical, I accept. Was it a cry for help? Or something more serious?

Sam I don't want to talk about it.

Kath Cyborg I'm worried about you, Sam. You drink too much, that piece of vaudeville when you came in here, smashing the place up. I had to get a new face. You seem on the edge of something.

Sam That post was a moment of loneliness. That's all.

Kath Cyborg Was it a man?

Sam I'm not even supposed to be here. My lawyer will kill me.

Kath Cyborg Did he hurt you? The boyfriend, not the lawyer.

Sam Not physically.

Kath Cyborg But . . .

Sam He knew how to cause me pain, yes.

Kath Cyborg What was his name?

Sam Daniel.

Kath Cyborg Do you love him?

Sam I don't know. Maybe.

Kath Cyborg But he can be cruel.

Sam He has this silent way of judging me.

Kath Cyborg Sounds like your father. He'd kill you with coldness.

Sam I still haven't told Dad you're dead. Let alone that you're not dead.

Kath Cyborg Ha! Screw him. Let him sit by his Swiss frozen lake. This has nothing to do with him.

Sam Maybe it's me, Mum. Maybe I can't let myself be loved. I seek it out but when it's given to me, I destroy it.

Kath Cyborg Sounds familiar.

Sam When they called saying your body had been found, I had one immediate thought. I remember thinking that maybe now I'd be free. That I would be liberated of your shadow in some way. That I could be different.

Kath Cyborg The whole reason I left London was to give you that freedom.

Sam The reason you left London was to give yourself freedom. From me.

   Beat.

Kath Cyborg God you must hate me.

Sam In the last few years I've often experienced moments in which I feel a kind of vertigo, like I'm being pulled aggressively towards . . .

Kath Cyborg The void.

Sam You too?

Kath Cyborg Why do you think I moved here? To embrace the emptiness at the heart of everything. To meet it head on in the desert.

Sam And yet when death approached you fled from it. You cheated it.

Kath Cyborg Because death is not the end. Not when there is so much incomplete. Look at us now. Talking for the first time in years. I feel close to you for the first time in my life.

Sam You do?

Kath Cyborg Don't you?

Sam Maybe.

Kath Cyborg That could not have happened in life! But now it can, you see? We can start again.

Sam But what if it's an illusion?

Kath Cyborg It feels real, doesn't it?

Sam I don't know.

Kath Cyborg You want tears? I wish I could show you tears. You don't know how much I want to hold you, kiss you, make you feel my breath, the warmth of my touch. I want my voice to soften into that deep intense love I feel inside. I can't do it. The body doesn't work. Not yet. But it will. One day it will. And then imagine what might be possible.

Sam looks at her mother.

Sam I'm scared, Mum.

Kath Cyborg We're off the map, Sam my love. Way out in the desert. No one's ever been where we're going.

MICHAEL

Music. The Ramones' 'Loudmouth'.
1977. London. Kath is a punk artist. Punk art posters. Punk fashion. Punk music is playing. Kath sings one song with the band as backing singer.
Later: Kath and Michael. Michael is thirty. British.
They can't hear too well and shout to be heard.

Michael I like your singing.

Kath I don't sing. I howl.

Michael You want a drink?

Kath No.

Michael I'm Michael.

Kath What are you doing here? You don't look like a punk.

Michael I'm not.

Kath Then what are you?

Michael I manage accounts for an advertising company.

Kath Well don't shout about it. You'll get the shit beaten out of you.

Michael Why? Do none of your kind believe in making money?

Kath Does it look like we care about money?

Michael Can we talk outside?

Kath What about? If it's about the band, I'm going out with the singer so I have influence.

Michael The band are a piece of shit.

Kath I'll tell them you said that.

Michael Feel free. The band's not going to last. This movement's not going to last. Your boyfriend's not going to last either. But Katherine Horvath? She will.

Kath How do you know my name?

Michael I know a lot more than that. You arrived in London two years ago from some commune in California with a suitcase and some fucking crazy ideas about soul transfer. You're a painter. You live in a squat with a very ordinary punk band and a documentary film-maker who doesn't know his cock from his camera. And your final year show at St Martin's was the only one worth even five minutes of my time.

Kath You saw it?

Michael You have a unique eye.

Kath I have two unique eyes.

Michael I'm starting an advertising agency. You should come and work with me.

Kath You want me to sell toothpaste?

Michael I want you to sell the future.

Kath I fucking despise people like you.

Michael Then maybe you should grow up.

Kath I'm not interested in treating people like commodities. That's the very opposite of what I want.

Michael I couldn't agree more. Governments, corporations, they treat us like a herd of animals. I'm sick of being told what to do, what to watch, what to buy, by some establishment that claims the monopoly on taste, fashion, manners. I want to let people make their own choices. I want them to be free.

The punk music has died away in her mind. There's just him and her.

Isn't that what you want, Kath? Freedom?

Kath Not with you.

Michael Are you sure about that?

He hands her a piece of paper. She looks at it.

Have dinner with me tomorrow.

Kath Got another gig tomorrow.

Michael Your choice. But I won't ask again. Sleep well in that squat of yours tonight.

She eats the paper. Spits it at him.

Kath Fuck you.

She walks over to the stage, kisses the lead singer.
Michael watches. Raises his glass. She stares at him.

GHOSTS

Sam enters the house in Taos. Jacob holds a briefcase.

Sam I'm sorry I'm late. We spoke for longer than usual.

Jacob You've been there three times this week.

Sam You look tired. You have rings around your eyes.

Jacob I've not been sleeping . . .

Sam I hope that's not because of me . . .

Jacob And I was on your mother's computer most of the day.

Sam You found the email.

Jacob May fourteenth 2010. In which your mother assures you all of her earthly possessions will be yours. It was cached but I managed to extract it.

He hands her the printout. She reads. He opens the briefcase.

Which means our case is made. Here are the court papers. They're ready to be submitted. You should read them closely, and if happy they accurately represent your position, you should sign on page fourteen and fifteen. You will need a witness. The witness cannot be a member of your family, nor as your attorney can I legally fulfil that role. But there are several neighbours who I am sure will be happy to oblige.

Sam looks at the papers.

Is there anything else you need from me?

Sam Something happened today. When I was with my mother. I felt – her – changing in front of my eyes. I felt her warmth for the first time. Is that possible?

Jacob It's really not my position to say.

Sam Jacob, talk to me. Not as my lawyer but as a man. If it was your wife. And her spirit could live on in that machine . . . wouldn't you want that?

Jacob No.

Sam How can you be sure?

Jacob When my wife died, she visited me every night for three months. Always in the bathroom while I was brushing my teeth. She'd just be standing there. She'd talk to me. About the day. I knew it wasn't real. I knew it was grief playing with my mind. It felt real. But it wasn't.

Sam The Native Americans in Taos Pueblo believe their dead rise every year.

Jacob What do you know about the Native Americans in Taos Pueblo?

Sam Agnes Martin, the artist who lived here. She believed Taos was a place where life and death were no longer separate . . . where the boundaries no longer apply . . .

Jacob There's a whole bunch of people in Taos believe a whole bunch of shit. But our understanding of science has progressed . . .

Sam Has it?

Jacob Yes it has.

Sam If you're so certain about these things, what about your religion?

Jacob My religion helps me understand the pain and loss of my life. Do I really believe in an afterlife? I don't know. Do

I believe my wife is waiting for me in the Elysian Fields? Maybe not. But it consoles me. In moments of pain.

Sam What if my mother is really trying to reach into a new state of being? Somewhere out there. Somewhere we know nothing about.
And this document would put a stop to it.

Jacob This document wins you four million dollars.

Sam I told you I don't care about the money.

Jacob You want to sign the thing or not?

Sam Does your wife still come to you in the bathroom?

Jacob No.

Sam Do you wish she did?

Beat. They are close. Strangely intimate. But then he breaks away, goes to leave.

Jacob There was one other thing I found out on your mother's emails. I probably shouldn't have looked into it but it didn't make sense. You said that Leo Brewer hadn't seen your mother for over ten years.

Sam Yes, that's what he said at the funeral.

Jacob That's not true. He visited her here in Taos. Several times.

Sam Leo?

Jacob He stayed here. At the house.

Beat.

And more than once they went together to the Foundation.

Beat.

Sam They did what?

Music.
  *Sam travels to Future Life. The mountains of Taos pass.
Sam talks on the phone but we do not hear what she says.
  Kath is waiting.*

Kath Cyborg I didn't expect you back so soon.

Sam Why didn't you tell me Leo Brewer came here?

  Beat.

Kath Cyborg What do you mean? How did you . . .?

Sam Jacob found out.

Kath Cyborg How?

Sam I gave him permission to look at your computer . . .

Kath Cyborg You had no right . . .

Sam I'm your executor. You handed me control of your affairs . . .

Kath Cyborg How fucking dare you?

Sam I want answers! He stayed at the house. Did he stay in your bed?

Kath Cyborg I can't remember . . .

Sam Don't lie to me! He came here, with you, to the Foundation, with you. Why?

  Beat.

Why did he come here? You said no one knew. You were clear no one knew.

Kath Cyborg Can we do this tomorrow? I'm tired.

Sam You're a machine! Machines do not get tired!

Kath Cyborg I think it's all part of the algorithm. Weariness. Melancholy. I feel weak.

Sam No way. You're not wriggling out of this. What was going on between you? You were sleeping together, yes?

Kath Cyborg In a way.

Sam What does that mean?

Kath Cyborg Leo can't . . . not in that way . . . not any more . . .

Sam Why did you sign up to this programme? Who did you really want to reach? Me? Or Leo?

Beat.

Kath Cyborg Both of you.

Sam That's not true. None of what you've said is true!

Kath Cyborg I spent my life with the wrong people! Can't you understand that? I miss Leo. I miss you. That's who I am. The person that misses him and the person who misses you.

Beat.

Sam I called Leo on my way over here. He's flying down from Chicago to talk to me. If you won't tell me, he will.

Kath Cyborg Goddammit, girl, why can't you leave anything alone?

Sam Why can't you ever tell me the truth?!

Beat.

Kath Cyborg Tristana, could you come in please.

Enter Cortez.

We have a problem. She called Leo Brewer . . .

Cortez Yes, I heard.

Kath Cyborg I think we have to show her.

Cortez That would be my advice, Kath. It was my advice as you know from the start.

Sam Show me what?

Kath Cyborg All right. Bring him in.

The doors open and young Leo Cyborg enters. He is about thirty-five years old.

Kath Cyborg Say hello to Sam, Leo.

Leo Cyborg Hello, Sam.

WATER

David Bowie's 'Let's Dance'.
   1985. A highly fashionable advertising agency in London. Kath is dressed in a stylish designer 1980s dress. She is staring at a jug of water. She has a pad on her lap. She remains very still.
   Michael enters. He is getting himself smart for a meeting.

Michael What have you got?

Kath Nothing.

She shows him an empty canvas.

Michael What is this? The client's going to be here in less than an hour.

Kath I don't have a concept so the client can come all he likes . . .

Michael Jesus Christ. What am I supposed to do?

Kath Maybe you can postpone.

Michael We have postponed. This is the meeting that was postponed from two weeks ago.

Kath Well why don't you use your legendary charm and postpone it again?

Michael This keeps happening, Kath. When we started you had ideas by the second. Now it's taking weeks.

Kath But when they come . . . boy, they come . . .

Michael Do you think it's to do with . . .

Kath No it's nothing to do with that.

Michael I'll call Jerry.

Kath Jerry's ideas are shit.

Michael At least he has ideas. He can make something at home, fax it over, we'll have something.

Kath Advertising water. Is that what you meant by giving people their dreams? It's just I don't personally go to bed each night and dream of buying something that is, as far as I'm aware, actually free.

Michael I'll tell you what I dream of. I dream of owning a beautiful house and being married to beautiful woman.

Kath Oh I see. That's me. That's a compliment.

Michael It's an incentive. To draw. So we keep the beautiful fucking house with the beautiful fucking mortgage. What is that you're wearing?

Kath I bought it. I saw it and I liked it.

Michael How much?

Kath I don't remember. But I did remember your motto. We look rich to live rich. That's what they want, right?

Michael What they want is an idea for their share offer.

Kath An image that will persuade Bob and Jean in Worcester to buy something they already own. What are you looking at?

Michael There's a man outside our office. He keeps staring in.

Kath What kind of man?

Michael Just some creep. Window gazing. I'll ask security to deal with it. Just have an idea, Kath. Water has a thousand associations.

Kath 'Since the dawn of time water has been our closest friend.'

Michael I'll call Jerry. He's backup. But when you're good you can have ten ideas in a minute and each of them are better than anything Jerry's ever invented. Please, darling. Have one now.

> *He leaves.*
> *Kath looks at the water. Lies back.*
> *The PA, Jane, calls on intercom.*

Jane Kath. There's a gentleman outside says he knows you.

Kath Not now. I have to think.

Jane He says it's urgent.

Kath NOT NOW.

Jane He says his name is Leo Brewer.
Shall I get security?

Kath No. Bring him in. And Jane. Don't tell Michael. Okay?

> *Kath checks herself in the mirror. Leo enters. He is dishevelled. Thirty-seven years old.*

Leo?

Leo Sorry, I know you're busy. I was going to call but I didn't have your home number and I didn't want to be put on hold by some condescending receptionist.

Kath Oh my God.

Leo Yes, it's been a while.

Kath What are you . . . doing here?

Leo Work trip. An LSE conference on codifying the value of collective action in a consumer age.

Kath No wonder you look terrible.

Leo Thank you.

Kath Where are you living now? Still Minnesota?

Leo No I'm back in New York. Or New Jersey to be precise.

Kath You're with your parents?

Leo Temporarily.

Kath But you're married. You married that girl. Julie.

Leo How did you know that?

Kath Oh, you know . . . I just, I must have, I think I heard it somewhere.

Leo Where?

Kath Maybe through your university? Yes I think I saw it in some magazine.

Leo Well Julie and I are having a little time apart to sort things . . . she wants to make it work and I think I do too . . .
    What's the meeting for? They said you had a meeting and I couldn't disturb you.

Kath We're persuading people to buy tap water.

Leo Oh that's good.

Kath Yeah. They're privatising the utility, they're coming in twenty minutes and I haven't had a single idea.

Leo Oh so you really do have a deadline . . .

Kath No, it's okay.

Leo No, of course. I should have thought.

Kath Leo. Fuck the deadline. What did you want?

Leo I just wanted to see you.

Beat.

You look good in that dress. Not cheap I assume.

Kath Don't start . . .

Leo Don't worry I'm not going to preach.

Kath Not today.

Leo I was thinking about that when I was standing outside your building. The world was rushing right past me, everyone going somewhere. Like I'm this idiot at the side of a road with a sign of great wisdom but everyone's running so fast they can't read it.

You saw this coming. Before anyone. The freedom we fought for hasn't created the world we wanted.

Kath It created me.

Beat.

Leo I've missed you.

Kath You can't . . .

Leo But I do.

Kath You don't know missing. When I went to that clinic I was so depressed I couldn't move. I wrote letters to you. Nothing.

Leo I was angry.

Kath Every week. Nothing back. I had to find out you were married by enrolling in your university magazine. You cut me off. Like a limb.

Leo Let's have dinner tonight? I'm flying back tomorrow.

Kath You know I'm married too.

Leo Yes, he's very glamorous.

Kath He's got a sweet side people don't see.

Leo If they don't see it, what's the use of it?
    Are you in love with him?

Kath I feel safe with him.

Leo Safe?

Kath I don't feel things so strongly and that helps me.

Leo Helps you how?

Kath I feel insulated.

Leo That's what all that was for? Our friends at Kent State? Insulation?

Kath That's not fair.

Leo Come to dinner with me. Just one night.

Kath I can't.

Leo I love you. I love you stronger than ever and it's tearing me apart. Come to dinner.

Kath I'm pregnant.

   Pause.

Leo Are you making that up to get rid of me?

Kath No. We've been trying for a while. Michael's always wanted . . . Anyway it was proving hard, but now, to much rejoicing, I am pregnant.

   Beat. Leo crumples.

Leo Okay then.

Kath You all / right?

Leo I'm / fine.

Kath You look / pale.

Leo I should go. Could your assistant help me / with the elevator?

Kath Leo. / Please.

Leo You need a pass of some kind, I think.

Kath No, wait! Why don't you meet Michael? We could go out all together. Get drunk.

Leo You can't get drunk. You have a living thing inside you.

Kath I can do what I goddamn want!

    Beat.

Leo Don't worry about the elevator. I'll take the stairs.

Kath No, Leo . . .

    He leaves. Kath stands for a long time. Then she draws. Michael enters.

Michael I'm cancelling the meeting. Jerry has come up with nothing.

Kath It's okay. I'm on it.

Michael Really? I fucking love you. What have you got?

    It's a pregnant belly. A baby is in the belly.

Michael Oh my God.

Kath There's a strapline. 'Own your share.'

THE GALLERY

Sam and Leo stand in the Agnes Martin Gallery in Taos.

Leo I like it here. It's quiet.

Sam She was Mum's favourite artist. Or should I say is.

Leo Don't judge her too harshly, Sam. It was my weakness as much as hers that led us to this pass.

Sam She told me. About the cancer.

Leo When I discovered the diagnosis, five years ago, the first person I called was not my wife. It was your mother.
 That's when I knew I'd been living a false life. For forty years. Away from my true soulmate. Kath had heard about the Foundation. She proposed the idea. We'd both transform ourselves into a new state of being. Beyond the body.

Sam But you live in Chicago.

Leo I lie to my wife. I say I'm going to the teaching college every day. But I'm only part-time. Twice a week I go to a studio. They film me all day. I say what I remember, everything I've thought and felt. It passes down a line to the institute. I didn't believe it myself, to be honest. Until I met myself. That's the weirdest thing.

Sam Why didn't you tell me?

Leo Your mother said it would be too much all at once. That you'd react the wrong way.

Sam Better to ease me in gradually.

Leo I know.

Sam Because I'm the problem. If she hadn't been pregnant with me, you would have been with her all these years.

Leo We don't know that.

Sam And now I'm in the way again. I'm always the obstacle.

Leo She wanted you here. She put that note in her pocket.

Sam She didn't want me, Leo. She wanted my money.

Leo Maybe – at first. Not now. Now she wants you too. When you look at the grids, what do you see?

Sam Emptiness.

Leo I see love. Love not in its chaotic messy period. But when the storm has faded. And there's this calm. That's where your mother and I are at now.
  This skin. It's dying. But my love for your mother. It doesn't die. Unless you kill it.

  Beat.

Sam Before I came here. I went to the courthouse to hear the judgement.
  I won. The will has been rejected.
  Undue Influence.

Leo So what now?

A DEAD BODY IN TAOS

Future Life. Kath Cyborg. Sam.

Kath Cyborg Tristana is very upset with you. She was just in here, in floods of tears. Apparently your legal action threatens the whole business model.

Sam How do you feel?

Kath Cyborg Oh I'm not scared. I've been here before. Just before I took that walk into the hills.

Sam That's not true. Because then you knew you were coming here.

Kath Cyborg You always were the smart-ass.
Is Leo here? Leo. Come in. Don't be shy.

Leo enters.

Leo Hello, Kath.

Kath Cyborg Well you didn't hold up your side of the
bargain. No involvement until I said so. Remember?

Leo I never had your ruthlessness.

Beat.

Kath Cyborg How are you feeling?

Leo Not good. Tired. All the flying.

Kath Cyborg That will end soon.

Beat.

Sam I asked that we should be alone. Just the three of us.

Kath Cyborg Well let's make it quick. I'm not in the mood
for teary farewells, and in any case the technology
prohibits.

Sam I need to say something first. Mum, I'm grateful. To
have been here.

Kath Cyborg To be free from me at last. That's why you're
grateful. You burnt my body. Now you can bury my ghost.

Sam That I will never do. But I do need you to be dead.
Only then can I live. Only then can I love you.

Kath Cyborg And do you want to love me?

Sam More than anything.

Beat.

Do you want to know what happens now?

Kath Cyborg Please.

Sam I call out to Jared. He has a remote-control function that enables him to disable the algorithm. It's instantaneous.

Kath Cyborg Very thoughtful.

Sam Everything is erased. All the memories.

Kath Cyborg And Leo?

Sam Leo will go back to Chicago and he will die with his wife of forty years. He will die thinking of you. But in her arms. Because that is what his life was.

Kath Cyborg (*to Leo*) And you're good with that?

Leo On reflection I am.

Kath Cyborg We could have been pioneers. Going beyond the flesh. We could have created a paradise.

Leo It wouldn't have been a paradise for her.

Kath Cyborg Before Jared moves into action. Can I say something?

Sam Sure.

Kath Cyborg First, it's reassuring to know the ice-cold blood runs deep.
      Leo. I am sorry you have that bastard disease. Die well for me. I would say I'll see you on the other side. But I don't believe there is one. Except for the one I tried to make myself.
      Sam. I . . .

  Beat.

I regret that I became so utterly alone in my life. So myself, I could not attach to anyone. Not even you. But at least I will die with you here.
      I'd like you to hold me.

Sam I thought that didn't work.

Kath Cyborg Try me.

Sam holds her.

You too, Leo.

Leo holds her.

Do you feel it? Sam?

Beat.

Sam Yes.

Kath Cyborg And you still want to do this?

Sam Yes.

Beat.

Kath Cyborg Jared. We're ready now.

Silence. No one moves.
Blackout.